ABC of Election Strategy

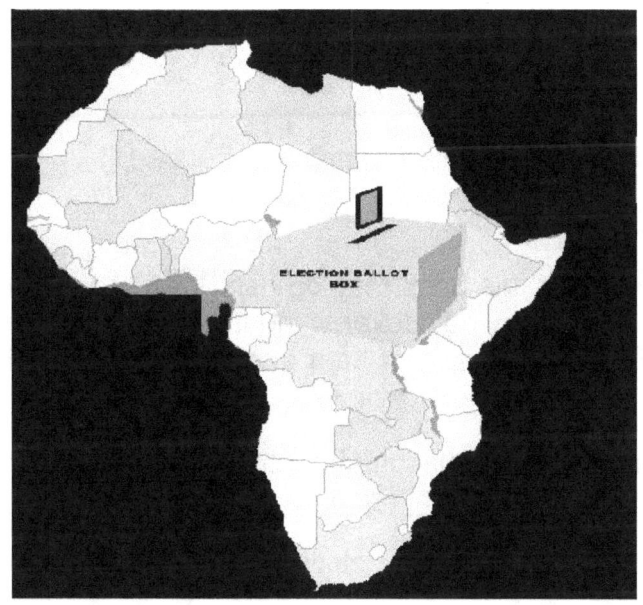

Tips For African Politicians To Win An Election, Play Safe & Remain Focused

This publication is designed to provide accurate and authoritative information in regard to the subject matter covered.

It is sold with the understanding that the publisher is not engaged in rendering legal or other professional service. If legal advice or other expert assistance is required, the services of a competent professional should be sought.

Printed in the United States of America

ISBN 978-1-4092-5568-0

For further information about the author contact him by email: info@temitopeolodo.co.uk

Also visit the website below:

www.temitopeolodo.co.uk

Second Edition

Figure 1 - Temitope Olodo speaking at Rivers State
House of Assembly Retreat

Forward

When I was asked to forward this book my initial thought was that politics is a dirty game especially in Africa. Though, my opinion was clouded by my personal experience as a political prisoner in The Gambia for 2 years following a military coup, it is still true to say that Africa politicians operate in what I would term an 'hostile environment'.

That said when I read this book; I agreed with the author that there is capacity within the African continent for politicians to operate an effective governance process but they would need to play safe and remain focused. I remembered when I was arrested and I had to send 'words' to my wife that I was still alive; it was worrying because I had no contingency plan to protect my family. It was like any normal day on the day of The Gambia military coup and even when the situation worsens, I had so much in my mind to think straight. However, this book creates food for thoughts and I was very lucky that my family was spared the ordeal I went through. Now, you can sit down with your family and understand how difficult situations would be handled strategically.

Whatever you do ensure that you read this book from cover to cover and have some plans in place to protect you and your family from harm whilst upholding the constitution you swore to defend.

Enjoy the reading!

Lt Col Ebrima Chongan (Rtd)

Former Assistant Inspector of Police

The Gambia

Content Page

DEDICATION

I dedicate this book to lovers of democracy across the continent of Africa.

Acknowledge

I will like to say a special thank you to all my colleagues in the civil enforcement industry that actually gave their precious time to add value to this masterpiece.

I am also in debt to all the numerous politicians that I spoke to in the course of writing this book and their constructive feedback.

Introduction

Many African countries in this decade have experience civil unrest following release of election results or mass demonstration post-election on the grounds of dissatisfaction with election malpractices or populace perception of election rigging.

The level of violence differs from country to country and it could be mere peace demonstration to uncontrollable widespread of civil unrest in certain countries that eventually lead to civil war.

In Kenya, the announcement of the election result in December 2007 led to political violence that resulted in the death of over 300 people within 3 weeks and over 50,000 people displaced (Source: BBC).

In Zimbabwe, the ruling party intensify its political prosecution of the opposition party and the election result held in early 2008 was not released until international pressure was mounted on the president and of recent, holding of an election even after the opposition withdrew from the exercise on the grounds of political intimidation was condemned by many countries around the world.

June 12 1993 remains a day in Nigeria history when the presidential election was cancelled and the presidential aspirant, Chief Moshood Abiola, was later arrested for treason.

Though, he died in prison prior to his imminent released by another junta regime, the cancellation of the result led to widespread political violence and many political commentators believe that the election was the most democratic exercise undertaken in Nigeria political history. His manifesto was unique because it was developed on the basis of changing concept of governing to concentrate solely on delivery for the people.

Today, some of the issues identified in the manifesto such as Primary Health Care and education remain urgent issues that the government is yet to tackle effectively. The violence that erupted after the 2010 election in Cote d'Ivoire led to the death of many people in that country and it is time African politicians learn to comply with democratic practices.

Thus, this book reflects on all the misgivings associated with election malpractices across Africa and provides over 100 political tips for politicians contesting an election to enhance their chances including how to be security conscious.

Election Planning Strategy

Planning for a successful political campaign and strategy

Membership

To be successful at election, the first thing that you need to do is to start building your membership base in your ward or constituent, you need to do this by making sure that you encourage and recruit enough members to join your political party, these members will be your foot soldiers during election. In your ward or area, it is the members that select the candidate that they like to represent them, therefore it is very important to familiarise yourself with ward members.

Advice Surgery/Regular Meetings

Advice surgery or regular meeting is very important because it will enable you to be close to your community and it will give you the opportunities to pick up issues in your ward, what are the concerns of your residents; the information gathered will be useful to put your party manifesto together. You can also use the information you gathered during your advice surgery to target your voters during THE election because you will be able to capture their names, address, email, telephone etc.

It is important that you understand that once you are elected you are available to see all members of your ward or constituent regardless of their political affiliation.

Electoral Register – Registration

The Electoral Register is the single most important document in any election campaign. Without it you will not know who is eligible to vote, therefore to whom your campaign should be addressed, You need to encourage your members to register to vote, being a member does not mean they can vote they need to be officially registered before they can vote during election. The period of compilation of register will vary from country to country but it is important that the register is up to date before election.

Manifesto

A manifesto is a published declaration of your party policies. You should consider producing a manifesto so that people can know what policies you have; it tells people what your priorities are This should not be left until the campaign starts and should be done in collaboration with party member to contribute to the manifesto. Your manifesto should include issues that are affecting people in your area where you intend to stand for election, as it will help you to campaign base on your policies.

Campaign

The purpose of any election campaign is to convince registered voters to vote for the candidate they prefer. This is the opportunity for you to convince voter to vote for you and there are different ways to achieve it.

There are different ways of campaign

Public Meeting

A Public Meeting is the meeting that is open to the public. This can take place in public venues such as Mosque, Church, library or community halls and sometimes schools. This can be use to find out opinion from our local area by inviting the public for a discussion. The format at these meeting is that there will be a neutral chairperson who will host the event and put questions to the candidates or invite questions from the audience and public meeting can be use to discuss a particular issue or issues such as school closures, more buses for your area, hospital closure or the maintenance of your housing estates. Public meeting can also be use to alert those residents that are affected mostly by the issue. If you are addressing a legitimate issue of local concern you may find that people who attend the meeting may join your campaign. You could also alert the local press to your public meeting and make sure the venue is accessible to those you wish to attend.

Canvassers

Canvassers are foot soldiers of politics from my experience as a local politician without the foot soldiers; it will be difficult to engage the voters. Canvassers are the only people from a political party that most of the public ever meet in person before election

Canvassers should be briefed before they canvass on what issues may be brought up on the doorsteps and what the candidate's/party's line on the issues are in the area. They should be equipped with canvass packs that should include all the necessary information that will help them to campaign in the locality

Leaflets

Election Leaflets are produced to enable you to enhance your profile, this will help people who may not know you or may have never meet you before. It is a way to publicise you and your party policies and campaign issues. You need to deliver the leaflets across your ward or constituent. You can use graphics, photos and graphs if appropriate. These fill space and are more likely to be looked at by voters than many paragraphs of written words.

Local Press

The local press are a wonderful channel for you to use to improve your profile as the community champion. Regular press release via radio, newspapers and TV saying what your campaign is all about; you should be prepared to write letters to the local press for publication in their letters page and be prepared to respond to similar letters from other candidates. If it is national campaign, it would be a good idea to consider the use of national TV and bill board posters for your campaigns.

Using New Technology for Political Campaign: Website, SMS/Text Phone

Technology can play a major role in winning election, having your own personal website or party website will enhance your chances of been seen by many people and your website is more than just an online collection of your campaign materials, it should be your link to the electorate 24/7.

Your website can act as a contact point for your supporters and you should have a section within it where people can leave their name, address and contact number or any information for you. It can also be an avenue for you to tell people what you are doing on a daily basis and how they can contact you in person. You also need to let people know how to join your campaign or how they can contribute to your campaign. You need to put our manifesto on your site in an easily accessible format that the public and your supporters can access including print off.

The people who you can't get to during your canvassing can at least see what you're up to via your site, the use of mobile phone, text/sms messages can reach up to 100% of campaign volunteers with mobile phones while Phone banking involves real people talking to real people. Twitter and facebook can change the outcome of an election by targeting the core voters. Facebook friends and Twitters can keep people updated on the progress of the campaign and can be used on Election Day to remind people to vote in conjunction with you knocking on their doors.

The use of phone makes it easy for volunteers to do phone banking from their own homes. This will be useful to let your target audience know that you are campaigning in their area and to let their friends know and invite them along. More people are now using phone and social networks as a means of engaging with large audience.

The Eve of Election

What you need to do at this stage is to prepare knock-up sheets. These are lists of the voters during your canvassing said that they were going to vote for you. This information is taken from the canvass returns from your door knocking. You will need to analyse the canvass returns and break your polling district into smaller areas that your door knocker can visit in one trip on the polling day. The area should be area that a person can walk around and the street should be close or adjacent to each other. This may be different from country to country, the most important thing is to know who your voters are and where they are, so that it would be possible to encourage them to go out and vote

Post Election

After the election, when the result is known whether you are successful or not, you will still have valuable information which will help you next time to campaign. The canvass results would have identified some of your supporters. The most important part of the information that you need to be able to find out is who actually voted in the election in your area. You can check the 'Marked Register' which is kept at the Electoral registration office of your local authority. You should be able to get a copy after the election. This marked register will produce an authoritative record of who voted and when you compare that with your canvass returns, it should produce a good but not perfect picture of who voted for you. This information is important as it will show over the course of several elections the voting pattern in your area.

Pre – Election Strategy

Ten Tips for Pre-Campaigning Strategy

1. Map Out Your Political Ambition

The first task for you as a new politician is to conduct a reality test and determine what actually you want, how to get it and what your future career aspiration is within the political scene. Joining politic with no prior knowledge and understanding of the mechanism involved or challenges ahead could make the journey difficult.

2. Research Political Party Affiliation

Many new politicians are normally invited by members of their families to join a political party and they are asked to take over to preserve a role associated with a pol-geographical area. However, where this is not the case then it is critical for a politician to ensure that he understands the vision of the party and make sure that he agrees with it in principles or rather that it aligns with his/her own convictions.

3. Meet with Political Party Officials

It is important that as a politician you meet with party officials and understand what the party stands for. Whilst, it is possible for the political party to have a visible manifesto, yet in practice you might discover that what they uphold and believe is quite different. So familiarise yourself which information about the godfathers of the party and decide if you can work with them and whether you can get the right footing in the party.

4. Build Up Your Team

From the onset, you need to select and build your team to ensure that you are ready for the task ahead. You need people with understanding and influence within the political circle to get you anyone you need to gain victory. Building is critical because if you surround yourself with people or individuals with a different mindset from you then you are working on a path of failure. A vision can be easily destroyed if the people around you have a different mindset and view things different from you.

5. Write Your Manifesto

You need a good manifesto and is good depend on whom your audience are, what they want and what is realistic. If you employ the service of a good researcher from the onset then it is easy for you to explain what you are hoping to achieve and get the person to sought information to support it. A manifesto is simply a declaration of your intention or what you intend to drive if voted into office.

There is nothing wrong to agreeing with your opponent manifesto and in fact, that will win you respect with followers of your opposition. As far as you can add other elements to your manifesto that indicate that you intend to deliver what you are saying.

6. Develop Your Media Strategy

A media strategy is needed from the time you decide to run for a political post because it serves as your check and balance, ensuring that you are focus on the goal and deliver the message you wants to convey. Your staff and political party need to understand what you stand for and what can be said or not said about your political campaign.

The media strategy also helps to frame your engagement protocols with the media.

7. Develop Your Public Engagement Strategy

Many politicians are good are engaging with the public during their first election campaign and normally find it difficult to win the same vote during their re-election because they lose focus. Public engagement is continuous and need to be done strategically from the first day in office until when you decide to retire from politics.

Different level of the public require different approach from the youth under the voting age to the adults, you need different mechanism to win them to your side.

8. Know Your Opposition

Never start your campaign without knowing everything there is to know about your opponent. Their family history, education background, philosophy and tolerance level. Yes! I mean tolerance level.

If your opponent is a violent person, then you might need to have a different strategy to address him to allow bloodshed and lost of someone close to you. Many Nigeria politicians have lost their lives for not understanding their opponent and making arrangement to address how to best tackle them.

9. Build your image

The way you portray yourself before your join politic or shortly about you join politic is a critical factor to your success. If in your community, you are known to be a nonsense person then that will follow you to the polling station on the Election Day because people will say that you are a person of principle. Thus, it is important to start thinking of the image you build before you get into politic or shortly after you enter into politic.

10. Help Yourself

Believe in yourself 100% and you need to be selfish. There are many people around you that would push you to do things with an interior motive. Ensure that you are 100% sure that what you are doing is for your benefit and in line with your vision.

Security Awareness For Politicians

Ten Ways to Protect Yourself & Family

1. Develop A Risk Matrix For Yourself & Family

You need to have proper security to protect you and your family from harm especially when you join politic. Therefore, the first thing you need to do is draw up a matrix to determine who is more expose to more risk in your family apart from you. When you have identified the person, then you need to develop a way of reducing that risk.

2. Produce A Security Contingency Plan

You need to produce a plan that addresses the risk identified following your assessment of the likelihood of harm against yourself and members of your family. The plan needs to be reviewed weekly, monthly or quarterly depending on the level of threat and the likelihood.

Your plan should cover areas such as:

SURVEILLANCE - operations can be urban or rural – if you have two homes that you use most frequently then your plan need to cover the two houses with security ingredients like CCTV etc.

TRAVEL SECURITY - Do you travel a lot? If the answer is Yes, then you need not just the guard that provide personal security but also travel security, which will include understanding how to activate your contingency plan if your security is compromised during your traveling.

Of recent, many politicians have been killed when traveling because this is the time they are most vulnerable especially with few security operatives at their disposable. In developed countries of the world, most of the public engagement of important politicians is not made available to the public apart from big public event. So, if you are the Minister of Transportation traveling from Accra (Ghana) to the next big city that is two hours away from the main capital by road, information about when you will be leaving should not be made available to the public nor should your entrance route be common knowledge.

RESIDENTIAL SECURITY – The common form of security that is visible when you talk about residential premises is "physical" security barrier to your property, which prevents unwanted persons from entering your property, but your security operatives plan should work both ways to cover inside and out, and provide a covert or overt presence as required.

ASSET PROTECTION - protecting small valuable items such as jewels & documents, through to artwork, boats, plant and other high value goods are critical. Your plan should cover your approach to protecting your asset in the event of any emergence and ensure you have "emergence money" that you and your family members could access very easily when it is required.

LOCATION AUDIT - The security of your facilities is essential to your operational success. Threats could come from a variety of sources ranging from political opponents to terrorist attack, your office may be targeted by a special interest group or criminal organisation, or your wife's office may have a less protective plan because it is remote and unprotected or the target might be where you hang out with the 'guys' after working hours etc.

You need to ensure that you conduct a location audit to ensure that all necessary security plans are in place to protect you from avoidable harm or danger.

A review of your security audit will examine your security position and objectives, and design and implement a comprehensive plan to mitigate the risks.

3. Improve Your Personal Security Plan

The worst thing a person can do is to surround himself or herself with people you have no knowledge of their history or tolerance level. You can be easily killed through your car driver or personal doctor. Do you know the financial state of your close friend or who is luring your maidservant to extract information about your where about?

4. Establish a Safehaven

Follow three basic steps in setting up a safe-haven in your home:

- Designate an internal room;

- Install a two-way communications system or telephone; and

- Furnish the safehaven with an emergency kit.

It is highly unlikely you would spend more than a few hours in a safehaven; however, the supplies listed below are suggested for your maximum safety. Your security advisor can tell you more about how to select and secure your safehaven.

The following is a checklist of possible safehaven supplies.

- Fire extinguisher
- Fresh water
- 5-day supply of food
- Candles, matches, flashlight
- Extra batteries
- Bedding
- Toilet facilities
- Sterno stove, fuel

- Shortwave or other radio
- Medical/first aid kit
- Other items for your comfort and leisure--a change of clothing, books, games

5. Improve The Physical Security Plan For Your Home

Normally, you should employ a security manager responsible for managing all your security issues and when you are away from home, he/she should ensure the following:

- Secure your home. Close and lock all windows and doors. Don't forget to lock garage or gate doors.

- Consider purchasing timers to turn on outside and inside lights automatically at various times throughout the night.

- Check outside lighting and replace older light bulbs.

- If you use a telephone answering machine, turn off the ringer on the telephone. If you don't have an answering machine, unplug or turn off ringers on all telephones.

- Lock all jewelry, important papers, currency, and other valuable portables in a safe place such as a safe deposit box or home safe.

- Ensure all personal and home insurance policies are up-to-date and that your coverage is adequate.

Residential security is a critical component of any personal security plan. The following guidelines should be used in reviewing your residential security.

- All entrances, including service doors and gates, should have quality locks--preferably deadbolt. Check your:

- Front Door
- Rear Door
- Garage Door(s)
- Service Door(s)
- Sliding Glass Door
- Gate
- Swimming Pool Gate
- Guest House Door(s).

- Don't leave keys "hidden" outside the home. Leave an extra key with a trusted neighbour or colleague.

- Keep doors locked even when you or family members are at home.

- Have window locks installed on all windows. Use them.

- Lock louvered windows--especially on the ground floor.

- Have locks installed on your fuse boxes and external power sources.

- If you have window grilles and bars, review fire safety. Don't block bedroom windows with permanent grilles if the windows may be used for emergency egress.

- If you have burglar or intrusion alarms, check and use them.

- Keep at least one fire extinguisher on each floor, and be sure to keep one in the kitchen. Show family members and household help how to use them.

- Periodically check smoke detectors and replace batteries when necessary.

- Keep flashlights in several areas in the house. Check the batteries often, especially if you have children in your home. (They love to play with flashlights!)

- A family dog can be a deterrent to criminals. But remember, even the best watchdog can be controlled by food or poison. Do not install separate "doggy doors" or entrances. They also can admit small intruders.

- Choose a location that offers the most security. The less remote, the safer your home will be, particularly in a neighborhood close to police and fire protection.

- Know your neighbors. Develop a rapport with them and offer to keep an eye on each other's homes, especially during trips.

- Establish safe family living patterns. If you understand the importance of your contribution to the family's overall security, the entire household will be safer.

- While at home, you and your family should rehearse safety drills and be aware of procedures to escape danger and get help.

- Educate family members and domestic help in the proper way to answer the telephone at home.

- Vary daily routines; avoid predictable patterns.

- Know where all family members are at all times.

Use these same guidelines while on leave or in travel status.

6. Vetting Your Staff

The worst thing you could ever do is to have people work for you that you don't know anything about them. In light of the current political violence and assassination across Africa countries politicians need to extend their vetting to increase financial profiling of their staff. Agencies in the developed world pay money into accounts of potential applicants or new staff to test their tolerance level and know if they will report to relevant authorities about the money.

7. Political Assassination

Some political opponents are using assassination as a means to get rid of politicians they do not like. The act of assassination occurs when someone important is murdered for one of two reasons:

- Political beliefs: the selective killing of an individual enemy in the hope that their policies die with them.
- Power: committed simply to take the place of a person, or to transfer their power to someone else. As international terrorist Carlos the Jackal put it: "To get anywhere, you have to walk over corpses".

Politicians need to be aware that they are likely target of political assassins and need to have measure to protect them from such action. More importantly, recent development as proved that political opponents are willing to attack family members to destabilize a politician.

8. Improve Your Safety in Hotels

Politicians are always on the move and are most vulnerable when they are outside their familiar territory. Therefore it is important that the following actions are considered when on trip and staying in an hotel.

- Do not discuss your business or travel plans in public areas where they may be overheard. Discuss your travel plans and movements during your stay with as few people as possible.

- Selecting a hotel room on the third to fifth floor generally will keep you out of reach of criminal activity or political assassins.

- Do not entertain strangers in your hotel room. Many politicians have died mysterious in their hotel room after entertaining female ladies etc

- Never leave valuables in your hotel room exposed or unattended, even in a locked suitcase.

- Place valuables money, jewelry, airplane tickets, credit cards, passport in a hotel safe deposit box or room safe.

- Familiarize yourself with escape routes in case of fire or other catastrophe.

- Use the door chain or bolt lock whenever you are in your room.

- Use the door viewer (peephole) before opening the door to visitors.

- Do not discuss your room number while standing in the lobby or leave your room key on restaurant or bar tables.

Keep your room neat so you will notice disturbed or missing items quickly.

9. Reinforce the security of your office

You need to keep a record of who is visiting you in the office and have effective record management system in place. You should also have an emergency excavation place, which there is a trigger of what is deemed to be life-threatening event.

10. Crisis Management

Crisis management is a critical aspect of your security plan and you need to know how you will respond to crisis and how your security advisor should escalate it. If you collapse for unknown reason and there is no plan in place to address the situation, you are at the mercy of the people is less understanding of what your precious life meant.

Ensure that there are protocols in place that tell people what to do and who is in charge. The same way your "will" tells everyone around that your property and life investment belong to your wife and children, so let your security strategy tell people around you who you trust to handle business when you are incapable of making that decision for a short while.

Family Disaster Plan

Eleven Things To Do When Creating Your Household Emergency Plan

1. Meet with household members and discuss the dangers of possible emergency events, including fire, severe weather, hazardous spills, political assassination attempt and terrorism.

2. Discuss how you and your family will respond to each possible emergency. Information saves life and what you discuss with your immediate family might be the only key to saving them.

3. Discuss what to do in case of power outages or personal injuries. If you don't have a

personal doctor assigned to you, get one to ensure that everything is in place.

4. Draw a floor plan of your home. Mark two escape routes from each room. Post emergency contact numbers near all telephones, pre-program emergency numbers into phones with auto-dial capabilities.

5. Teach children how and when to dial the emergency assistance number and how to make long-distance telephone calls if you are out of the country.

6. Pick a friend or relative that all family members will call if separated (it is often

easier to call out-of-state during an emergency than within the affected area.

7. Instruct household members to turn on the radio for emergency information.

8. Pick two meeting places:
   - A place near your home.
   - A place outside your neighborhood (or off-island) in case you cannot return home after an emergency.

9. Teach them the basic First Aid and how to prepare a Disaster Supply Kit

10. Keep family records in a water and fireproof safe. Inexpensive models can be purchased at most hardware store.

11. Family Disaster Plan Testing – Make sure you test the plan once quarterly or every six month to ensure that it is understood and lesson learnt incorporated with the plan.

Disaster Supply Kit

Ten Things To Include In Your Kit

Preparing a Disaster Supply Kit ahead of a foreseeable time can save precious time. You should consider including the following items in a Disaster Supply Kit.

1. At least one week supply of water (1 gallon per person per day). Store water in sealed, unbreakable containers. Replace every 6 months.

2. At least one week supply of non-perishable packaged of canned food and a non-electric can opener.

3. A change of clothing, rain gear, and sturdy shoes.

4. Blankets, bedding, or sleeping bags.

5. A first aid kit and prescription medications (be sure to check the expiration dates)

6. An extra pair of glasses or contact lenses and solution (be sure to check the expiration dates)

7. A list of family physicians, important medical information, and the style and serial number of medical devices such as pacemakers.

8. Special items for infants, the elderly or family members with disabilities.

9. Identification, credit cards, cash, and photocopies of important family documents including home insurance information.

10. An extra set of car and house keys. Thinks of tools such as screwdrivers, cutters, and scissors; duct tape; waterproof matches' a fire extinguisher' flares' plastic storage containers' needle and thread' pen and paper; a compass; garbage bags; and regular household bleach.

Political Assassination

Ten Ways To Avoid Political Assassination

Political Assassination is the targeted killing of a high-profile person. However, there are ways to escape assassination and below are ten ways to do so.

1. Increase the numbers of guard that protect you and ensure that they have range of skills.

2. The use of armored cars or armored limousines with modern versions rendering them virtually invulnerable to small arms fire and smaller bombs and mines.

3. Bulletproof vests also began to be used, though they were of limited utility, restricting movement

and leaving the head unprotected - as such they tended to be worn only during high-profile public

4. The use of double identity – lookalike person to attend event.

5. Numerous different checks before being granted access to the official or attendees to an event you are attending.

6. Use of alternative route of travel

7. Avoid travelling to unfamiliar venue or territory

8. Use of intelligence information to access security risk

9. Have good relationship with the security agencies

10. Avoid travelling at night

Political Kidnapping

Thirteen Tips to Avoid Kidnapping

1. When in your car, always keep the doors locked. Any time you drive through areas with negative profile then be weary.

2. Leave ample maneuvering space between your vehicle and the one in front of you. If you are approached by suspicious persons while you are stopped, do not roll down windows; drive away quickly.

3. If you are being followed by another vehicle that is suspicious, try to find the nearest police station, hotel, or other public facility. Once you find a place of safety, don't worry about using a

legal parking space. Park as close as you can, and get inside fast.

4. If another identified vehicle tries to force you to pull over or to cut you off, keep driving and try to get away. Try to note the license plate number of the car and a description of the car and driver. If this effort places you in danger, don't do it. The information is not as important as your safety.

5. If you are being followed, never lead the person back to your home or stop and get out. Drive to the nearest police station or public facility.

6. If you are traveling alone and a car "bumps" into you, don't stop to exchange accident

information. Go to the nearest service station or other public place to call the police.

7. Never, ever pick up hitchhikers or stop for a pretty lady on the road. It could be a trap!

8. When you park, look for a spot that offers good lighting and is close to a location where there are a lot of people. Lock valuables in the safe place and lock all doors.

9. Extra precautions are necessary when shopping. If you take packages out to lock them in your car boot, then plan to return to the stores to do more shopping, it may be a good idea to move your car to another section of the parking lot or street.

10. If you have car trouble on the road, raise your hood. If you have a radio antenna, place a handkerchief or other flag there. When people stop to help, don't get out of the car unless you know them or it's the police. Ask the "good Samaritan" to stop at the nearest service station and report your problem.

11. If you are in a parking lot or parked on the street and have trouble, be wary of personal assistance from strangers.

12. Sure that your security advisor is aware of your travel plans and you have contingency plans for unexpected challenges.

13. Avoid using the same route all the time.

By using these basic safety tips and your own common sense, you can help protect yourself.

Political Manifesto

Ten Ways To Write An Effective Manifesto

How to Write a Manifesto

A manifesto is a document that sets down all the views and opinions that a political party has on certain issues and it will tell the reader the ways that the party would change these issues if they were elected as the government.

On an individual basis, a manifesto is what the candidate would try to do for the people he or she represents in the country if they were elected. To write your own manifesto for your party, you will need to decide which issues you are going to concentrate on. To write your manifesto, follow the steps below:

1. Choose some issues, either that you think are important or maybe that the main political parties have as issues in their manifestos.

2. Try to have at least one local issue, one national issue and one international issue

3. Test the manifesto with a controlled group to ensure its relevance

4. Label them on the basis of their importance and think about what the voters might see as the main issue.

5. Make provisions to accommodate changes to the issues if you were to be elected. These are your policies. Be clear about your opinions on the issues but don't make promises that you can't keep – for example free transportation without considering the impact on budget.

6. Write up your issues for publication

7. Develop your strategy for selling your manifesto idea to the public

8. Select your audience and your distribution strategy

9. Monitor the acceptance of the manifesto by the public and evaluate the response to your manifesto

10. Be ready to amend or change your manifesto if needed

Public Speaking

10 things that can destroy your public image

It is a lot easier to damage a brand than it is to build one. You can grow a brand gradually over time but the same brand can be destroyed over night.

If you are not consciously caring for your brand you are probably damaging it. Try and avoid doing the following:

1. **Inconsistency** – Through your words and behaviours you make yourself a brand, thus make sure you remain consistent. Make sure your brand is not making promises it cannot keep.

2. **Short term thinking** - You have to think long-term with branding otherwise you make a decision that might look good but in the long

time would adversely impact negatively on your brand.

3. **Lack of focus** – As a politician, you need to avoid doing things that confuses your followers and gives the media an ammunition to present your brand as not focus and sure of its stands on issues.

4. **No charisma** - Your brand need to be visibility and distinct.

5. **Too negative** – Avoid being driven by bad news and have something positive to say otherwise you will destroy your brand.

6. **Bad spoken grammar** – Learn the act of public speaking and do not use words that you are not familiar with.

7. **No substance** – Do not waste time on issues of no substance to you or your career because it would destroy your brand.

8. **Lack of leadership** - Lead from the front and you do not have to be a dictator to gain respect. Lack of leadership can destroy a brand very quickly.

9. **Carelessness** – Ensure you are alert and avoid slander because it would destroy your brand.

10. Me, Me, Me. Enough about Me, what do you think about Me? Your brand lives in the brains of your readers, customers and prospects. **It's not all about you**. If you make it all about you they will find a replacement that is all about them. Answer "What's In It For Me". It's that simple.

Military In Politics

Nine ways to keep the military away from politics

1. Equip the Police

Equip the police force with the necessary weaponry to match any military coup d 'etat.

2. Intelligent Capacity Improved

Civilian government should ensure that there are at least three intelligence chiefs reporting to the Presidency and the police intelligent capacity is developed to grant leverage.

3. Anti-corruption crusade intensified

The battle against corruption must be focus and robust to international standard with evidence of adhering to due process. With that in place, it would be difficult for the military to organise a coup to change the government of the day.

4. Reform the Police

A reform of the police as a neo-military capacity or as a paramilitary creates a balance with the community or nation.

5. Professionalism in the Military

The civilian government need to support and encourage the military to be profession and this would help them to concentrate on their primary objective.

6. Negotiate with another country

Sign a treaty with another country to intervene if the military interrupts civilian administration.

7. Empower the Military

Empower the military to participate in regional and international assignment such as ECOWAS, African Union and United Nation Peace Missions.

8. Avoid Internal Political Conflict

Internal political conflict would definitely trigger military intervention and politicians need to be extra cautious.

9. National service for all school graduates

Ensure that you create an atmosphere that discourages military involvement.

Political Debates

Eight political debates that you should avoid

1. Religious Debates

Do not participate in religious debates because as a politician you are expected to be neutral and represent all faith groups.

2. Tribal Conflict Debates

Tribal conflicts are sensitive issues and politicians can easily be dragged into the issue and it is bad for political career.

3. Politician Integrity Debates

Because you are standing head up today does not mean that you do not have skeleton in your cupboard. Avoid getting involved in the criticism of colleagues in the political scene that are found wanting.

4. **Salary Debates**

Some politicians destroy their political career by debating the salary of critical vote winner in a manner than make them No. 1 public enemy. Always be on the side of the populace and shout louder on welfare reform issues rather than salary cuts.

5. **Military Debates**

It is true that the military are no longer in power in most African nations but they are still powerful and politicians must always be on the right side of them. If there is a coup and you are known to them to be an antagonist of the military then you are first of the list to be dealt it. Be wise!

6. Equal Opportunity Debates

There are issues that you might have difficulty with as an individual but ensure that it does not cloud your judgment when participating in political debates. You need to be an advocate of equal opportunity in your public outward looking role as a politician.

7. Constitutional Reform Debates

Whilst reform is a good thing to participate in, many veteran politicians would tell you that reform to do with extending the duration of the presidency stay in office or increase politician benefits are not good debates to participate in.

8. Family Values Debates

Many electorate want politicians to feel their pains and legislates on good values but not engage in senseless debates of family values to make a point. So if you can, avoid a family value debate that would end of pitching you against the electorates.

Back Cover:

This book highlight issues that politicians need to consider in dealing with their electorates, political godfathers and opponents.

A compilation of information obtained from years of discussion with politicians that cut across the African continent and information available in the public domain.

The author in this book explores the things that politicians need to do to make them acceptable to their electorates and respected by their political rivals. Whilst politics in certain African countries is deemed as a 'dirty game' there are exciting things about it that makes it attractive.

Endorsement:

"….Excellent book and a must read book for any upcoming politician…"

Olusegun Oyewole, Publisher and Author of "Bush in God's Hand"

"…..Excellent masterpiece and a must read for all lovers of Democracy……"

Adeola Babatunde Esq., Publisher and Author of "Pathway to Success"

About the Author:

Temitope Olodo is a political scientist with international recognition for his numerous articles on African politics and he is author of the widely read book "The Rules of Engagement" and former Publisher of **The Integrity Magazine (UK)**.

He holds two Bachelor degrees in Political Science (BSc) and LLB Law with a Master degree in Human Resources from London South Bank University.

A highly prolific and charismatic speaker, Temi's experience spans the public, private and voluntary sector with specific interest in African Diaspora matters, project management and strategic community engagement.

He was a voluntary special constable with the UK Kent Constabulary Police and worked in the civil enforcement industry for many years.

Relevant Publications:

Description:

Understanding the concept of religious freedom is essential for policy writers, faith practitioners and more importantly anyone eager to engage with the faith community. An effective faith engagement and implementation strategy must take account of the legal development in the field of religious discrimination.

This author takes the readers on a journey that provides an explanatory legal etymology of the concept of religious discrimination within the international scene and the United Kingdom before the arrival of HRA 1998.

This book also examines
protections available in
other common law
countries like USA,
Australia, Nigeria and
South Africa.

For more information visit -
www.lulu.com

Description:

It is now an acceptable fact that community engagement is vital for successful delivery of public-orientated policies and the author in this book provides the readers with the tools to achieve the task.

Tapping into a wealth of experience developed over the years, the author explores the concept of community engagement from continent to continent and shares that information to guarantee effective community cohesion.

ISBN 978-1-4092-5568-0